Readalongs

Punchinello

A traditional song
Illustrated by Margaret Power

Look who is here!

Punchinello, funny fellow.

Look who is here!

Punchinello, funny man.

What can you do,

Punchinello, funny fellow?

What can you do,

Punchinello, funny man?

We'll do it too,

Punchinello, funny fellow.

We'll do it too,

Punchinello, funny man.

Who will you choose,

Punchinello, funny fellow?

Who will you choose,

Punchinello, funny man?

Look who is here!

Punchinello, funny fellow.

Look who is here!

Punchinello, funny man.

What can you do,
Punchinello, funny fellow?
What can you do,
Punchinello, funny man?

We'll do it too,

Punchinello, funny fellow.

We'll do it too,

Punchinello, funny man.

Who will you choose,

Punchinello, funny fellow?

Who will you choose,

Punchinello, funny man?

Look who is here!

Punchinello, funny fellow.

Look who is here!

Punchinello, funny man.

What can you do,

Punchinello, funny fellow?

What can you do,

Punchinello, funny man?

We'll do it too,

Punchinello, funny fellow.

We'll do it too,

Punchinello, funny man.

Who will you choose,

Punchinello, funny fellow?

Who will you choose,

Punchinello, funny man?

Look who is here!

Punchinello, funny fellow.

Look who is here!

Punchinello, funny man.

What can you do,

Punchinello, funny fellow?

What can you do,

Punchinello, funny man?

We'll do it too,

Punchinello, funny fellow.

We'll do it too,

Punchinello, funny man.